GUIDE TO GRANTS WRITING FOR NON-PROFITS

Harriet Grayson

Ocean Breeze Press

RI

Guide to Grants Writing for Non-Profits

Harriet Grayson

Published by Ocean Breeze Press

Rhode Island

Manufactured in the United States of America

Library of Congress Cataloging-in-Publication Data Grayson, Harriet.

Guide to Grants Writing for Non-Profits

GUIDE TO GRANTS WRITING FOR NON-PROFITS / Harriet Grayson

TABLE OF CONTENTS

CHAPTER 1

Introduction to Grants: Private, Corporate & Government

Variety of sources for grants but not all sources are equal

Grants are awarded by a variety of sources including private and family foundations, corporate foundations and government (i.e., federal, state, local). The largest grantor is the federal government, which gives the vast majority of its grants to state governments and the major cities in the country. Large, well-established non-profits can and do receive grant funding directly from the federal government. However, small and mid-size non-profits are more likely to receive government funding from the states or cities. Non-governmental grants awarded by private and corporate foundations are a very important source of grant funding for all non-profits.

Private Foundations have a revered place in American philanthropy. Recognizable families in American industry have created private foundations bearing their names. During the nineteenth century, it was industrial giants such as Carnegie, Rockefeller, Alfred Sloan, and Ford. In the late twentieth century, it was names associated with new technology: Gates, Dell, Hewlett, Packard, Verizon and Genentech.

During the last 150 years, banking families and the companies they created have started major private foundations with names such as Mellon, JP Morgan Chase,

Wells Fargo, and Bank of America. More recently, pharmaceutical firms have emerged as major grantors and include household names such as GlaxoSmithKline, Pfizer, Abbott, Lilly, Johnson & Johnson, Bristol-Myers-Squibb, Merck and Novartis.

The Carnegie, Rockefeller, Ford and Mellon Foundations are no longer associated with the families of the great barons of industry that created them and are no longer managed by the families. Foundations created in the latter part of the last century such as the Gates Foundation are managed by family members and their priorities reflect the interests of the family.

The largest foundation in the country is the Bill & Melinda Gates Foundation, headquartered in Washington State, with global interests awarding grants totaling more than $3 billion. No other US foundation is even close in size as determined by its total assets. The next largest, in terms of grants awarded, are pharmaceutical companies that provide patient access programs: GlaxoSmithKline, Abbott and Pfizer.

How likely is it that a small non-profit will receive grant funding from these grantor giants? A very small opportunity exists although never completely impossible if the organization has an extraordinarily interesting program or project. Big foundations, as well as the federal government, are drawn to big projects usually operated by organizations that have been in existence for many years and serve a large population. The strategy for small and mid-size non-profits is to collaborate with a large non-profit if the goal is to receive a grant from either the federal government or a major foundation.

Private Family Foundation

Most family foundations are small compared to the Gates Foundation. There are thousands of them in the country. A wealthy charitable couple or individual, who are not necessarily multimillionaires, start their own family foundation usually on the advice of a lawyer. An estate lawyer will probably recommend that any private family foundation start out with an asset base of $2 - $3 million. There are tax benefits for creating a private family foundation. It can minimize a wealthy family's estate tax liability. It avoids capital gains tax on the sale of appreciated propriety or stock assets by contributing them to the foundation. Family members are usually involved and may serve as the Executive Director and/or members of the Board of Directors. It is a grand ego booster assuring that the family's name continues into perpetuity.

Private Family Foundations receive tax benefits and therefore must meet certain financial requirements such as distributing at least 5% of its assets each year to public charities. That means a typical private family foundation with assets of $2 million is distributing approximately $100,000 in grants. For small non-profits (less than $1 million operating budget) these private family foundations are a valuable source of grant funding. But unlike the government, disbursements and information about selected organizations is not needed to be known to the public (transparent). There is no requirement that private family foundations share their decision-making or rationale for their choices.

Where do non-profits find out about private family foundations and who runs them? There are two ways to research private family foundations.

First, look around your community and identify the wealthier members. These may not necessarily be the richest people. Look for the newly highly successful entrepreneurs who more likely to fund a private family foundation because they value the tax benefits and ego boosting prestige that comes with the creation of this legal entity. Read the local newspapers and magazines (paper or online editions) and see what names appear at local fundraisers or are mentioned as being donors. Most non-profits in promoting their own events will list business and corporate donors. Check out those names and companies as potential grant donors. Also check with area estate lawyers. No lawyer is going to reveal any confidential information, but they may let you know who has started a private family foundation.

Remember that a private family foundation is obligated by federal IRS law to distribute at least 5% of its assets each year so unless they are donating all their funds to only one organization, there is opportunity. Also, most foundations are funded exclusively or in part with publicly traded stocks and bonds. So when the "Market" is doing well, the assets in all these private family foundations is swelling offering greater opportunities.

Consider marketing to private family foundations the way a non-profit organization approaches any wealthy donor. The key is to identify the family member that controls or manages decision-making by the private family foundation. Personal connections and familiarity are the keys to successfully being awarded a grant from a private family foundation. They do not operate with the same rules and formalities that govern other types of foundations (with the exception of the largest family foundation in the country the Gates Foundation, which operates like a large business).

The second and perhaps most important source of information on all foundations is The Foundation Center, headquartered in New York City on Fifth Avenue, with offices around the country. This is the premier source of information on foundations around the world. The Foundation Center researches and compiles information on almost all foundations ranging from the smallest to the largest. Its information is available in two formats: first,3 hard copy directories and second, online subscription services. Nothing is free but most large public libraries, college & university libraries and state libraries usually purchase the hard copy directories and/or subscribe to the online services. The Foundation Center's online subscription services offer a variety of plans, which vary based on the amount of foundation information being provided. The most expensive plan provides information on all the foundations in its collection while the least expensive provides information on only the larger foundations. The online services are updated regularly while the hard copy directories are published annually. Unless the organization is going to constantly apply for foundation grants, it is not economically advantageous to subscribe to the online service or purchase an annual directory. A monthly trip to the library is probably better use of money and time.

Private Foundations

The number of American foundations is more than 100,000 with assets approaching $600 billion. The greatest number are small foundations with assets under $1 million but more than 2,500 foundations have assets in excess of $25 million.

All these foundations are headquartered across the country in every state. Most small and mid-size foundations have a preference for funding projects and programs in their own neighborhoods. The smaller foundations are less likely to fund projects that are nation-wide although large foundations will fund smaller projects that have national significance and can be replicated in other parts of the country.

In today's world of online shopping and banking, there is also a similar trend towards online grant submissions. Many foundations now operate their own web sites. The application process is explained on the web site as well as the submission process often using templates with drop-down menus. It's usually simple, which makes it highly competitive since even more applicants can submit. Sometimes the online submission is the first step and the foundation will review its many applications. Then it chooses a few for a more elaborate submission, which is then mailed or emailed to the foundation.

If the foundation has its own web site there are usually online guidelines. These include deadline dates, which must be followed, and areas of interest. Foundations are managed and directed by an Executive Director and/or a Board of Directors. In each case, these individuals will develop priorities that they wish to fund. Priorities do not last indefinitely and change over time sometimes as a result of changes in the Executive Director or the Board of Directors.

With online grant submissions, there are often templates that make it easy to write the grant. Compose the grant section from your own computer. Then it's a matter of cutting and pasting the section into the allocated space on the application. Usually, the template provides instructions including the maximum number of words, which must be absolutely followed. Otherwise, the template will not accept the submitted section. Often a submitted budget can be one developed on spreadsheet software such as "Microsoft Excel" from your own computer and then uploaded onto the application.

All foundations, even the smallest, have activities or things that they will not fund. Examples of restrictions include construction, operating expenses (i.e., utilities, rent, supplies), fundraising activities, lobbying, etc. If the foundation has a web site, these restrictions may be explained.

Corporate Foundations

Most publicly traded corporations in the country operate foundations. Companies that no longer exist still have functioning foundations that bear their names such as Gimbel's and B. Altman's, now defunct New York City department stores. Corporations that are not publicly traded may have charitable giving units rather than a separate legal entity called a foundation. They still award grants.

In all cases, these corporate foundations are more about themselves than they are about just making contributions to non-profits. The corporation seeks opportunities that make the corporation look good and improve their public image. As a result, corporate foundations tend to stay away from anything controversial. They seek projects and programs that have more of a "feel-good" attitude, more uplifting and positive.

The guidelines reflect the corporation's area of interests. There are always restrictions regarding what the corporate foundation will and will not fund. Typically, they do not fund construction or operating expenses, fundraising or lobbying activities. Corporate foundations tend to focus on youth and economic development projects. Also they focus on projects that correspond with what the corporation manufactures or sells. For example, pharmaceutical companies' foundations tend to focus on health issues.

Every major retailer has its own corporation foundation. They can be easily researched by doing an internet search. Some retailer foundations have their own web sites but are usually accessed through the main corporate web site. These corporate retailer foundations use simple, online drop down menus as the vehicles for submitting the grant applications. They have easy to follow directions but are highly competitive. The amounts awarded tend to be in the $5,000 - $25,000 range and are usually for only one year. There can be time restrictions about reapplying for a grant by a non-profit. If the organization is rejected by a corporate foundation, they may have to wait at least 12 or 24 months before reapplying.

A community bank or credit union foundation is the best grant funding source for a small to mid-size non-profit. They are reliable, often distributing funding quarterly. They focus on the local community and their application processes tend to be simple. Community bank and credit union foundations, with their modest grant awards (often $5,000 or less), look to make a big impact with limited funding. A smaller non-profit can be greatly assisted with a modest grant award.

Start by seeking grant funding from the bank or credit union where the non-profit does business. Just like being in business, a non-profit should expect some reciprocity. In fact, a non-profit should expect reciprocity from all its vendors from the plumber to the insurance broker.

There are two great research sources for information on corporate foundations. First is the internet. Using an internet search engine such as Google, search and see which retailers and other businesses are in your community. Then go online and look for these corporate foundation web sites. In the case of a bank or credit union foundation, the Executive Director or Board Chair should directly speak to the bank manager beginning with the financial institution where the non-profit banks.

Second, The Foundation Center in New York City (www.foundationcenter.org) is the other important source of information. Again, a local large public library is the place to start for obtaining information from The Foundation Center.

IRS Form 990

Most tax exempt organizations, including non-profits and foundations, have to file the IRS tax form 990. Family foundations file IRS tax form 990-PF. The IRS Form 990 provides a wealth of information.

The following information that is reported on IRS 990 is important:

Contact Information

- o Name & address of the foundation
- o Name of Executive Director and Board of Directors

Grantees

- o List of all organizations that received grants
- o Address of all organizations receiving grant funding
- o Amount received by each grantee
- o Usually brief description of each grantee or title of project/program awarded funding

Why is the above information important? First, if the non-profit intends to submit an application, the relevant contact name and address is available. Second, by listing the Board of Directors, a non-profit can discover if someone in the non-profit organization knows these people. Always remember it's not *what you know but who you know*.

More importantly, it demonstrates the real interests of the foundation's decision makers regardless of what may be stated elsewhere. Are the programs/projects or non-profits that received grants seem to meet the foundation's guidelines as written on the foundation's web site or found in The Foundation Center information? They don't always, because a foundation board member or Executive Director may have a personal relationship with the grantee organization and the mission of the grantee organization may not match the foundation's area of interests. Someone in the foundation's decision making hierarchy likes a particular organization, its mission, staff or board members and that organization receives funding.

Review the grant amounts that are listed. That is significant because a non-profit can quickly observe the minimum and maximum grant awards. If you then proceed to submit a grant application to this foundation, keep in mind the amounts – don't go higher but also don't go too much lower.

What is the geographic distribution of the grant awards? This is important because usually small and mid-size foundations make awards to organizations that are physically close to the foundation's headquarters. But a non-profit's location is not always within close proximity because a board member or the Executive Director of the foundation may have a specific interest in an organization outside of the geographic area of the foundation.

What to remember

Every non-profit that has been in existence for at least one year should be considering applying for foundation grants. If the non-profit can find an intern that likes to spend their days with eyes affixed to a computer screen, let them search the internet for foundation information.

CHAPTER 2

Government as a Friend

At all times the Government provides grants to Non-Profits

You may already know that the United States government has billions of dollars to distribute in the form of grants to non-profits. You probably just don't know how to get your share of it. Governments on all levels offer grants to non-profits: federal, state, county, city and town plus quasi-government agencies such as transportation and housing authorities.

Practically everybody is eligible to apply for government grants. This includes non-profits of all sizes and governance such as community-based organizations, colleges and universities, professional, occupational and trade associations, and faith-based organizations.

The availability of federal grant funding is part of a larger political and economic cycle. The amounts fluctuate as do the priorities, but billions are still available from every federal agency which then makes it available to the states.

The big news was the arrival in 2009 of monies through "stimulus funds", otherwise known as the American Recovery & Reinvestment Act. The act was proposed by President Barack Obama and appropriated by the US Congress in early 2009 to the tune of almost $800 Billion. The money has been spent but the US Congress continues to argue about the need for further large-scale federal stimulus to fix and build the nation's roads and bridges, transit systems, bike paths and pedestrian walkways.

These federal funds are available through an open competitive process, which increasingly relies upon a sophisticated online system currently used by more than 26 federal agencies. The system is designed to streamline an otherwise cumbersome process. In fact, most federal agencies are moving towards an exclusive on-line system although some agencies require both an on-line application and the mailing of supportive documentation such as audited financial statements and letters of support.

Traditionally, most government funding is linked to budget cycles usually reflecting the fiscal accounting cycle of the originating agency. For example, the federal fiscal year begins October 1st. Therefore many federal funding application deadlines, as well as the release of funding are tied to that fiscal cycle. A grant application referring to federal FY2015 means that the funding cycle begins October 1, 2014 and ends September 30, 2015. State governments operate on a different fiscal cycle; likewise grants are more likely to be announced and rewarded based on the state cycles. All but four states run their fiscal years from July 1 to June 30. The four exceptions are: New York and Texas which run their fiscal cycles from April 1 through March 31st, and Alabama and Michigan operate their fiscal cycles identical to the federal fiscal cycle, October 1 through September 30th.

Sometimes what happens is that there are more favorable applications than there is money available. So applications can receive passing grades from government reviewers but not be funded due to a lack of money. The result is the non-profit may indeed be sent an award letter and then later another letter indicating that the application would have been funded had additional funds been available.

Suggestion -- never hire or enter into a contract with a vendor or purchase expensive equipment based on a favorable review or receipt of an award letter unless the non-profit actually receives a signed contract from the originating government agency.

Free Money – Don't be Deceived no free lunch

There are endless promotions seen on TV and the internet, heard on the radio and sometimes to be found in the classified sections of newspapers proclaiming free government grants available. This is all hype and verges on fraud. Yes, government grants are available but they are not that easy to get and they all come with strings attached. To protect the taxpayer's money, your money, the government doesn't willy-nilly give away funds. The money is not for the taking. However, if your non-profit has a good idea that fits within the guidelines provided by the grantor agency, practices sound accounting methods, employs experienced staff and can submit on time and within page limitations a reasonable grant application, then government grant funding is possible. It's not simple but it's possible and the more a non-profit submits applications, the more likely they will eventually get funding. More submitted applications is better than less. Practice makes perfect. And success breeds success. Once the non-profit has received that first grant contract, has established a record of sound accounting and documented performance standards, the next government grant becomes that much easier to obtain.

Opportunities: RFP – PA - RFA

A RFP (Request for Proposal), Public Announcement (PA) or RFA (Request for Application) are the most commonly found grant opportunity announcements. However, government agencies do use other terms. The federal Department of Housing and Urban Development uses the term Notices of Funding Availabilities (NOFA). Other examples: the federal Department of Justice requests "Solicitations" while the federal Environmental Protection Agency may announce RFIP (Request for Initial Grant Proposals) because many of their initial announcements are used as screening devices. The non-profit submits a first application and a majority of those applications are rejected. Those remaining applicants then submit a more detailed application for the actual funding. State agencies may simply refer to a grant opportunity as a PA (Program Announcement).

Researching Grant Opportunities

There are good online sites to look at for grant opportunities, but there is no one site that lists them all. The federal government has become more technologically sophisticated in recent years so that a variety of RFPs, PAs or RFAs can be located on the major federal grant site – www.grants.gov. The federal government's Federal Service Desk for the above web site operates 24 hours a day, 7 days a week except on Federal holidays. The number is 800-518-4726. Never hesitate to ask for help. Your tax money pays for the service.

The Centers for Disease Control and Prevention (CDC) announced in May 2005 that their entire grant funding opportunity announcements will be available through www.grants.gov. However, not all agencies are so committed to this practice. Most states are not as organized so there are a myriad of sites for locating state and local funding.

In addition, state and local governments use newspapers to make grant announcements. Scrutinize the larger circulation newspapers in your community under the "Public Notices" section for RFPs.

Federal Government

The largest funding source in the United States is the federal government. The majority of grant opportunities are awarded to non-profits that have previously received federal funding. However, the federal government is always seeking to expand its list of grantees, if for no other reason than it looks better politically. In fact, the federal government has created special categories of awards directed to new entrants called "Seed Money" grants, those for non-profits with small budgets (under $300,000) and those in existence for fewer than three years. It is unlikely for a brand new non-profit (under one year) to receive federal grant funding because an important element in a successful award is demonstrated fiscal responsibility. The federal government determines this by reviewing the non-profit's financial statements.

All non-profits should start reviewing federal funding opportunities by clicking on the federal web site www.grants.gov. More than 1,000 different grant programs and more than $500 billion in annual awards are awarded through this system. The largest federal agencies are represented on this site including: Department of Agriculture, Commerce, Defense, Education, Health & Human Services, Housing & Urban Development, Justice, Labor, Transportation, National Science Foundation and FEMA. However, one should never assume that this site has all grant opportunities listed, so it is always advisable to also directly search the web site of specific federal agencies such as Health and Human Services (HHS) or Housing and Urban Development (HUD), which operates 35 programs and authorized $1 Billion in grants last year. These are very large federal agencies with multiple levels of agencies under these behemoths. It is equally important to search out grants directly announced by sub-agencies.

For example, HHS is the largest federal agency and is the parent of 11 big and important grantor agencies:

- Administration for Children and Families (ACF)Administration on Aging (AoA),

- Food and Drug Administration (FDA)

- National Institutes of Health (NIH)

- Centers for Disease Control & Prevention (CDC)

- Agency for Healthcare Research & Quality (AHRQ)

- Agency for Toxic Substance & Disease Registry (ATSDR)

- Health Resources & Services Administration (HRSA)

- Indian Health Services (HIS)

- Centers for Medicare & Medicaid Services

- Substance Abuse & Mental Health Services Administration (SAMHSA)

Contact Your Federal Representatives

The next important step in successfully obtaining government funding is to better understand the federal granting bureaucracy by seeking out your non-profit's federal representation in the US House of Representatives and the US Senate. It's easy and extremely valuable to know who these men and woman are for the non-profit's financial well-being. For the US House of Representatives go to www.writerep.house.gov and locate your representative. The drop-down menus are simple to follow. First, indicate the state or territory, enter your zip code and, this is a must, the 4-digit code extension. If you don't know this 4-digit code extension number go to the United States Postal Service's web site for the information: www.usps.gov.

Find the local staff person that is a contact point. Most Congressional representatives have very fine and responsive local staff that is there to assist with constituents' problems and questions. If your non-profit is unknown to the district office staff, invite them to your offices and let them see or learn about what contribution your non-profit is making to the community. Ask the Congressional staff in the district office if they have suggestions of contact people in federal agencies and specific web sites to utilize regarding grant opportunities. The US House of Representatives is known as the "People's House" because they are more likely to be approachable than is the US Senate.

However, don't neglect to contact your US Senators. The web site is www.us.senate.gov. Use the drop-down menus to locate your non-profit's two Senators. Each Senator has his/her own web page and search it for the local staff person. Also, if the Senator is a Chair of an important Senate Committee or sub-Committee that impacts your non-profit's mission or services locate a staff contact to discuss future grant opportunities. Most Senators and Congress people have created e-mail newsletters. In some cases, these newsletters announce grant opportunities. Be sure to sign up for all available newsletters.

Getting Started

While the federal application process appears daunting, it is largely the completion of a series of forms followed by the creation of a project narrative and the development of a budget with a budget justification. Almost all federal applications start with Standard Form 424 - SF 424 (frequently revised but always the latest is available through the on-line application system), which is known as the Application for Federal Assistance.

In order to complete this form, your non-profit has to have accomplished several other steps along the way. First, your non-profit needs an Employer Identification Number (EIN) assigned by the Internal Revenue Service. Second, your non-profit needs a DUNS identification number or Data Universal Number System provided by the commercial credit rating company Dun and Bradstreet (D & B). This is a recent requirement. It's easy to obtain. Call 1-866-705-5711 or register on-line. The web site is http://fedgov.dnb.com/webform/displayHomePage.do. Be careful about obtaining a DUNS number because it should always be FREE. There should be no costs associated with obtaining this identification for use in applying for federal government grants so use the contact information listed above, and don't search the web for assistance in obtaining the number.

The Form 424 requires listing the Congressional District of the applicant as well as where the project is located. Usually a grant announcement has a title and an accompanying Catalog of Federal Domestic Assistance Number (CFDA). You must include this number on the Form 424. Also, the Form 424 requests a geographic description of where the project will be located – city, county, state, etc. As part of the documentation for any government grant application, it's always advisable to include demographics and if possible, a map delineating the physical geography of the project.

Other Forms

The federal government wants assurances that your non-profit follows the restrictions, regulations and laws that have been enacted. Standard Form 424B is the "Assurances – Non-Construction Programs." This form is an all-in-one legal promise that your non-profit can fulfill all the requirements of the particular grant you are seeking. It demands that the non-profit comply with all Federal statues regarding nondiscrimination. The language of Form 424B speaks to federal laws such as Title VI of the Civil Rights Act of 1964, Title IX of the Education Amendments of 1972, Section 504 of the Rehabilitation Act of 1973, Age Discrimination Act of 1975, Drug Abuse Office and Treatment Act of 1972, Comprehensive Alcohol Abuse and Alcoholism Prevention, Treatment and Rehabilitation Act of 1970. This language is standard legalese and should not present any problems; however, if your non-profit has been cited for discrimination, then you should consult your attorney and review carefully the language of these assurances.

Other issues addressed in Form 424B include compliance with the federal Hatch Act limiting political activities of employees: Davis-Bacon Act sets labor standards, environmental standards under a series of federal laws and the catch-all phrase: "Will comply with all applicable requirements of all other Federal laws, executive orders, regulations and policies governing this program." Unless your non-profit has been cited for violations under federal law, the only important assurance that you must be prepared to accept is the non-profit's willingness to meet required financial and compliance audits in accordance with the Single Audit Act of 1984. In other words, be prepared, and expect to be audited by the federal government.

The "Certifications" Sheet is similar to Form 424B. It contains language concerning five certifications or what can be referred to as declarations. "Certification 1" refers to debarment and suspension. This certification asks if the non-profit been debarred, suspended, declared ineligible for federal funding because of fraud or some other criminal act. "Certification 2" deals with maintaining a drug-free workplace. "Certification 3" concerns the prohibition against lobbying. "Certification 4" certifies that all the statements given are true, complete and accurate. "Certification 5" refers to maintaining a smoke free environment.

The issue of lobbying is important for the federal government. In addition to the Certifications Form there is a specific form called the "Disclosure of Lobbying Activities," which must be completed.

A private, non-profit organization must be prepared to demonstrate evidence of their non-profit status. The easiest proof is to provide a copy of a valid Internal Revenue Service 501c(3) Letter of Determination.

Applying On-Line

The government application process has joined the twenty-first century, permitting a number of federal agencies to accept grant applications electronically. However, there is a registration process that must be followed. Again, these are not difficult steps, but it does demand thinking ahead of the deadline. There are five steps to follow. The process for each step varies and can take from one day to two weeks so plan well in advance to submit an electronic federal grant application. It all begins with the applicant going to the appropriate web site: Start at the following: www.grants.gov/applications/get_registered.jsp. Also it is highly recommended that you "Take the Tutorial" and if necessary listen and take notes several times. There are also downloads of the information.

Step 1: Obtain DUNS Number

This is easy and referred to earlier because without a DUNS number you can't even fully review potential grant opportunities. The federal government has adopted the use of DUNS numbers as their way of tracking the federal grant allocations. It takes no more than one day to accomplish this step. Can be done on-line or via the phone.

DUNS Number registration requires the following:

- Name of the organization/non-profit

- Phone number

- Name of the CEO/Executive Director of non-profit

- Legal structure (corporation, partnership, proprietorship, non-profit)

- Year the non-profit started

- Primary line of business/non-profit services

- Total number of employees (full and part-time)

Step 2: Register with SAM (System for Award Management)

The on-line system requires an applicant to register with SAM (recent change as of July 2012; in the past non-profits registered with CCR). This registration process takes from 2-3 days to up to 2 weeks. If this is a first time applying for federal grants highly recommended to participate in the SAM Webinar.

SAM requires the following information:

- Name, email address, phone number, country

- Other information is asked but not required (full street address)

- Then the non-profit creates a username and password which cannot be changed

The process starts by going to web site: https://sam.gov. Click on Create an Account. In doing so, the non-profit designates an E-Business Point of Contact (E-Biz POC). This is an important selection for the non-profit so choose the individual wisely. It is the E-Biz POC who is authorized to designate or revoke an individual's ability to submit grant applications on behalf of their non-profit via www.grants.gov. A non-profit should consider a senior level financial officer. Only one person per organization can be designated the E-Biz POC. This person will then identify a special password called the "M-PIN." The M-PIN allows the E-

Biz POC authority to designate which staff member(s) are authorized to submit electronic applications through www.grants.gov. Staff permitted to submit applications are known as Authorized Organization Representatives (AOR). This process can take five business days.

IMPORTANT: Your non-profit needs to renew this SAM registration annually. You cannot continue to Step 3 without an up-to-date SAM registration.

Step 3: Username & Password

The person authorized to submit grant applications, the AOR needs to complete an on-line profile and create a username and password, which will serve as their "electronic signature." Without completing this process a non-profit cannot submit electronic applications. If the non-profit is small, the E-Biz POC and the AOR can be the same person although it requires an alternate email than the one used to register as a E-Biz POC.. After your non-profit registers with SAM, AORs must wait one business day before completing their profile. Once the profile is submitted that same day the AOR should be able to use their username and password.

Step 4: AOR Authorization

Once the AOR has registered, the E-Biz POC will receive an e-mail notification from Grants.gov. and an e-mail copy is sent to the AOR. Then the E-Biz POC must login to Grants.gov (using the non-profit's DUNS number for the username and the M-PIN password – process described in Step 2) and approve the AOR. This is the official step that permits the AOR to submit applications for the non-profit. Only the E-Biz POC can approve AORs. For large non-profits the AOR is probably a staff member but for smaller non-profits the AOR can be a consultant. Just be prudent in designating AORs. Immediately after the E-Biz POC logs-in and approves the AOR, the person can begin submitting grant applications.

Step 5: Track AOR Status

The AOR can track the status of their authorization by logging in to Grants.gov using their username and password (obtained through the process in Step 3) and learn whether the E-Biz POC has approved their authorization.

This may seem like a cumbersome process but it is really very useful if your non-profit intends to apply for multiple grants with agencies that are listed. Eventually, all federal agencies will be on this system. Remember there is a Help Desk 800-518-4726 and go back to the tutorial if you are confused or uncertain.

State Government

Ordinarily, the federal government will award $500 billion in grants to state and local governments. Although the federal government directly awards grants with the largest monetary amounts, non-profits are more likely to receive direct funding from their state government. The federal government makes significant awards directly to state government agencies for the purpose of distributing these monies to local governments and community-based organizations. As a result, non-profits residing in states where state government agencies are the most aggressive about getting funding from the federal government are more likely to obtain funding. Some federal government funding to states is based solely on population; therefore, the most populous states receive the most funding. In addition, certain federal monies are targeted to states with high levels of poverty, therefore non-profits in these states are more likely to receive funding for programs targeting the poor and disadvantaged.

Your best source of information about these federal awards to state government is your federal representatives: US House of Representatives and US Senators. Check with their offices on a regular basis.

As organized as the federal government has become in creating electronic services and easy researching tools, states are far behind in this modernization process. It is tricky and difficult to quickly locate state grant opportunities. Some state agencies are better equipped than others. The first step is simply to proceed to your state's official home page on the Web. Chapter 3 discusses the nuances of state government funding.

County Government

The country is divided into more than 3,000 counties in 48 states (Louisiana divides its state into parishes and Alaska into boroughs). Across the country, large counties receive direct funding from both the federal and state government for most programs. New York City is a combination of five counties while Los Angeles is the largest county in the country with a population of almost ten million.

In turn, the county governments make funds available through RFPs to non-profit community organizations. Each county operates in its own distinct style and using its own procedures. The best advice is to locate the official county web page and check the announcements every few weeks. The process of securing county government grant funds is highly variable; however, it is easier to establish relationships with county agency officials so it's important to find contacts at county agencies.

City Government

Large cities do make funding available that they receive from state and federal sources. It can be difficult to break into these systems because of long-established relationships, especially if the political officials have been in power for many years.

One source for general information on cities is www.statelocalgov.net. Depending on how much data is provided by the sources, it may start as the first step in an investigation of possible competitive RFPs.

One city-centered organization that does provide funding for programs is the National League of Cities (www.nlc.org). This is a good source to consult about potential grant opportunities.

Reviewing the RFA - Eligibility

This is the first issue to be addressed by a potential applicant. Am I eligible? Ordinarily, this should be a very easy question to ascertain. The RFP has a specific item on its announcements. The "Eligible Applicants" or "Eligibility Information" section lists who can apply.

Common eligible entities are:

• State agencies

• Units of local government

• Non-profits with 501(c)(3) IRS status

- Non-profits without 501(c)(3) IRS status

- Institutions of higher education

- Hospitals

- Libraries and museums

- Faith-based organizations

- School districts

- For profit businesses

However, the non-profit may have to check with another government body to confirm its eligibility. Sometimes the definition of eligibility is multi-layered. For example, a recent state of New York Education Department RFP stated, "In order to be eligible to apply for these grants, an organization must be a consumer controlled, not-for-profit 501c(3) with a governing board that is comprised of fifty percent or more people with disabilities. The governing board must be the principal policy setting body of the organization." Before moving forward on this grant opportunity, an organization either has such a board in place or can quickly establish a board with these specific requirements. There is no point in submitting an application if your non-profit is ineligible.

Geography

Certain RFPs are released for specific geographical regions. The federal government has ten regions and RPF's are announced that cover only specified regions, sometimes only a specific state is mentioned so only potential awardees located in these geographic areas should apply. Carefully read any announcements to ascertain if there are geographic limitations.

10 Federal Regions

Region 1: CT, ME, MA, NH, RI, VT

Region 2: NJ, NY

Region 3: DE, DC, MD, PA, VA, WV

Region 4: AL, FL, GA, KY, MS, NC, SC, TN

Region 5: IL, IN, MI, MN, OH, WI

Region 6: AR, LA, NM, OK, TX

Region 7: IA, KS, MO, NE

Region 8: CO, MT, ND, SD, UT, WY

Regions 9: AZ, CA, HI, NV

Region 10: AK, ID, OR, WA

Location matters in other ways. Certain federal grants such as those awarded by the Office of Justice, (US Department of Justice) pre-determine locations where the funding can be awarded based on crime statistics or where "pilot" or "seed" programs have already received initial funding. In a similar way, certain health grants are awarded to locations where there is a high incidence of certain health problems. So before embarking on an elaborate plan for completing an application, check these other factors. Does your non-profit's project reflect meeting the required statistics?

In RFPs that have a research element there may be other eligibility requirements. For example, federal research grants require that the applicant's principal investigator(s) – PI demonstrate the necessary research and academic credentials. To successful compete for this funding, the application must clearly show this fact, usually with a carefully constructed resume or curriculum vitae (c.v.). If the application requires a specific type of training; for example, completion of a course by the Centers for Disease Control & Prevention (CDC) then the resume must reflect this training.

The government also emphasizes collaborations. Part of an eligibility clause in the RFP may be a statement about demonstrating the existence of a board, partnership, memorandum of agreement between groups. If this collaboration doesn't exist or cannot be created in time for the submission, then don't attempt to submit an application.

Letter of Intent (LOI)

In the RFP announcement, there can be a statement about submitting a Letter of Intent (LOI) prior to filing an application. Submitting an LOI is not a binding obligation by an applicant to submit an application. But there are certain advantages for doing so. For some government agencies, the LOI is meant as a means of determining the level of interest of prospective applicants. In most cases, the LOI is nothing more than a statement that the organization is interested in the RFP. If there is more than one type of proposal announced, then the applicant is asked to check a box indicating interest in Component A versus Component B or interest in both parts of the RFP. Usually, the grantor agency actually provides a sample LOI and it can be faxed or sent by e-mail.. It's that easy.

However, in some cases the grantor agency may use the LOI as a way of culling through many potential applicants. It will be much more than a sample letter but several pages in length outlining the proposed project or program. In those cases, the LOI is mandatory and requires the applicant to have a solid idea about the prospective application. Review the requirements concerning the LOI carefully. It may state categorically that without submitting an LOI, a non-profit is prohibited from later filing an application.

It is always advisable, even if there is no requirement to file a LOI, to go ahead and submit one. It is not a binding document, so if the non-profit chooses later not to submit the LOI, it's fine. It usually doesn't take too much time and it immediately puts your non-profit on the agency's mailing list so that any changes to the RFP or modifications will be sent to your non-profit.

Deadlines are Crucial

The above statement cannot be emphasized enough – deadlines are crucial. Observe not only the day a grant application is due but also the time of the day. Deadline times can be listed as end of the business day – you need to find out what time that is. More commonly a specific time will be on the RFP. Typically these times are either 4 or 5 PM, but they can be noon. Most federal agencies are located in the Eastern Time zone so if your non-profit is on the west coast make certain that application is received on time.

Letters of Intent have deadlines which also must be respected. Forwarding backup documentation is sometimes required on a RFP. These requirements can have different deadlines but usually the timetable is within two weeks, no longer than 30 days after submitting the actual application. The easiest way to discard prospective applicants by the grantor agency is the failure of the non-profit to submit the application on time. One of the great virtues of on-line applications is that there are no postal or private delivery service complications. However, computers can fail so that's why even in a world of on-line applications it is most desirable to submit the application at least two days in advance of that deadline.

CHAPTER 3

State Government: Grants & Vendor Opportunities

State Nuances

State government is one of the most important sources of funding for non-profits of all kinds. There are two ways to view state funding opportunities. First, states issue RFAs soliciting grant applications in a fashion similar to what the federal government does. In fact, a non-profit is more likely to receive direct funding from a state agency than the federal government. Much of the money that flows to state governments is directly from the federal government for the purpose of distributing the money to local entities. This means that all the intricate financial accounting required when obtaining direct federal government money remains the same in accepting state money. State government agencies are audited by the federal government and likewise state auditors review the financial records of local non-profits receiving funding from them.

The best first step is to search for grant opportunities from state government agencies that most likely have a purpose which aligns with the non-profit's mission. However, state web sites are often quite confusing and it can be difficult to find a listing of state agencies. Also grant opportunities are sometimes listed as part of a state's procurement programs so it takes some time to maneuver through the site to find useful grant information.

Become a Government Vendor

Second, state governments offer extensive contracting and bidding opportunities that are available to non-profits beyond what is offered through the state grants system. This is a neglected source of potential revenue. Non-profit organizations should actively seek to learn more about the contract and bidding opportunities in the states where they operate. Non-profits think of government contracting opportunities as paving roads and repairing bridges but bids are 'let' for services such as conducting surveys, providing after school tutoring, mentoring, etc. As more state and local governments decide to privatize traditional government services, new opportunities have arisen for non-profits to compete for contracts. In addition, governmental and quasi government agencies such as historical commissions, housing authorities, water boards also offer grant and vendor opportunities.

Listing by State of official state web sites, state agency information links and vendor opportunity links

Alabama

www.alabama.gov (Alabama Agency and Organization Listing)

Division of Procurement, Department of Finance

http://purchasing.alabama.gov

Vendor Registration

http://purchasing.alabama.gov/pages/vendors.aspx

Disadvantaged Business Enterprise (DBE) Program

www.dot.state.al.us/bureau/hr/dbe/default.asp

Alaska

www.alaska.gov (My Government)

Department of Administration, General Services

www.doa.alaska.gov/dgs/

DBE Program

www.dot.state.ak.us/cvlrts/directory.shtml

Arizona

Az.gov (State agencies Directory - az.gov/app/contactaz)

Department of Administration

www.azdoa.gov/agencies/spo/business_resoruces.asp

ProcureAZ eProcurement System

https://procure.az.gov/bso/

DBE Program

www.azdot.gov/azdbe/index.asp

Arkansas

www.arkansas.gov (State Directory)

Department of Finance and Administration

www.dfa.arkansas.gov/Pages/default.aspx

Vendor Services

www.ark.org/vendor/index.html

DBE Program

www.arkansas.gov/adfa/programs/dbep.html

California

www.ca.gov (ca.gov/casearch/agencies.aspx)

Procurement Division

www.pd.dgs.ca.gov/default.htm

Contracts Register

www.eprocure.dgs.ca.gov/default.htm

Small Business & DVBE services – small business/disabled vets (state program)

www.pd.dgs.ca.gov/smbus/default.htm

DBE Program

www.dot.ca.gov/hq/bep/

Colorado

www.colorado.gov (State Agencies)

Department of Personnel & Administration

www.colorado.gov/dpa/dfp/spo/index.htm?opendocument

Vendor Registration

www.gssa.state.co.us/VenRegister

DBE Program

www.dot.state.co.us/EEO/DBEProgramPage.htm

Connecticut

www.ct.gov   (State   Agencies   -
ct.gov/ctportal/cwp/view.asp?)

Department of Administrative Services

www.das.state.ct.us/Purchase/New_PurchHome/B
usopp.asp

Contracting   Portal   to   search   for   Bid/RFP
solicitations, contract

www.das.state.ct.us/Purchase/portal/portal_home.a
sp

Minority & Small Business Set-Aside Program
(state program)

www.state.ct.us/das/Purchase/SetAside/SAProgin.
htm

Delaware

www.delaware.gov   (List   of   Agencies   -
delaware.gov/topics/agencylist)

Government Support Services

http://gss.omb.delaware.gov/contracting/index.sht
ml

Office of Minority & Women Business Enterprise (state program)

http://omwbe.delaware.gov/certify.shtml

DBE Program

http://deldot.gov/information/business/dbe/index.shtml

Florida

www.myflorida.com (Find an Agency)

Florida Purchasing Division

http://dms.myflorida.com/business_operations/state_purchasing

Florida Office of Supplier Diversity (state program)

http://dms.myflorida.com/other_programs/office_of_supplier_diveristy_osd/

DBE Program

www.dot.state.fl.us/equalopportunityoffice/

Georgia

Georgia.gov (Agencies)

Department of Administrative Services

http://doas.ga.gov/StateLocal/SPD/Pages/Home.as px

Vendor Registration

http://doas.georgia.gov/Suppliers/Pages/Home.aspx

Minority Business Enterprise Certification (state program)

http://doas.georgia.gov/Suppliers/Pages/SupplierM BE.aspx

DBE Program

www.dot.state.ga.us/doingbusiness/dbePrograms/Pages/ default.aspx

Hawaii

www.hawaii.gov (Agencies)

State Procurement Office

www.spo.hawaii.gov/

Hawaii State & County Procurement Notices

http://www4.hawaii.gov/bidapps/

DBE Program

http://hawaii.gov/dot/administration/ocr/dbe

Idaho

www.idaho.gov (Agency & Topic Index - idaho.gov/agency/agency_a.html)

Department of Administration

http://adm.idaho.gov/purchasing/

Vendor Registration

http://www.sicomm.net/

DBE Program

www.itd.idaho.gov/civil/overview.htm

Illinois

www.illinois.gov (State Agencies - www2.illinois.gov/pages/agencies)

Sell 2 Illinois – Business Registration

http://sell2.illinois.gov/

Small Business Set-Aside Program (state program)

http://sell2.illinois.gov/SBSP/Small_Businesses.htm

DBE Program

www.dot.il.gov/sbe/dbedir.html

Indiana

www.in.gov **(Find an Agency)**

Department of Administration

www.in.gov/idoa/2354.htm

Minority & Women's Business Enterprise (state program)

www.in.gov/idoa/2352.htm

Iowa

www.iowa.gov (Agencies – Skip to Content – Department Listing)

Iowa Business and Regulatory Assistance Network

http://regassist.iowa.gov/home.html

Vendor Registration

http://das.gse.iowa.gov/procurement/vendor_reg.html

Targeted Small Business (SB) Certification Program (state program)

https://dia.iowa.gov/tsb

DBE Program

www.iowadot.gov/contracts/contracts_eeoaa.htm

Kansas

Department of Administration

www.da.ks.gov/purch/

Vendor Registration

www.da.ks.gov/purch/VendorRegistration.htm

DBE Program

www.ksdot.org/divadmin/civilrights/

Kentucky

Kentucky eProcurement

https://eprocurement.ky.gov/

Vendor Registration

https://emars.ky.gov/online/vss/Advantage

DBE Program

http://transportation.ky.gov/Contract/DBE/

Louisiana

Procurement & Vendor Information

www.louisiana.gov/Business/Do_Business_With_t he_State/

Vendor Registration

http://wwwprd.doa.louisiana.gov/osp/lapac/vendor/Vnd rmess.asp

DBE Program

http://www8.dotd.louisiana.gov/UCP/Home.aspx

Maine

Procurement & Vendor Information

www.maine.gov/portal/business/vendors.html

DBE Program

www.maine.gov/mdot/disadvantaged-business-enterprise/dbe-home.php

Maryland

eMaryland Marketplace

https://ebidmarketplace.com/default.asp

Vendor Registration

https://ebidmarketplace.com/venlogon.asp

Small Business Reserve Program (state program)

www.smallbusinessreserve.maryland.gov

DBE Program

www.mdot.maryland.gov/MBE-Program/Index.html

Massachusetts

Procurement & Access Information System

http://www.comm-pass.com/

State Office Minority & Women Business Assistance (state program)

www.somwba.state.ma.us

Michigan

Buy Michigan First

www.michigan.gov/buymichiganfirst/

Minnesota

Minnesota Materials Management Division

www.mmd.admin.state.mn.us/mn02000.htm

Vendor Registration

www.mmd.admin.state.mn.us/webven/

Targeted Group/Economically Disadvantaged (TG/ED) Small Business Program (state program)

www.mmd.admin.state.mn.us/mn02001.htm

DBE Program

www.dot.state.mn.us/civilrights/dbe.html

Mississippi

Mississippi Electronic Portal Government Contracts

www.mscpc.com

DBE Program

www.gomdot.com/Divisions/CivilRights/Resources/Programs/DBE/Home.aspx

Missouri

Office of Administration Division of Purchasing & Material Management

http://oa.mo.gov/purch/

Office of Supplier & Workforce Diversity (state program)

http://oa.mo.gov/oswd/

Montana

General Services Division Procurement & Vendor Information

http://gsd.mt.gov/business/default.mcpx

DBE Program

www.mdt.mt.gov/business/contracting/civil/dbe.shtml

Nebraska

Administrative Services- Materiel/Purchasing Division

www.das.state.ne.us/materiel/purchasing/

DBE Program

www.dor.state.ne.us/letting/dbeinfo.htm

Nevada

Department of Administration – Purchasing Division

http://purchasing.state.nv.us/

DBE Program

www.nevadadbe.com

New Hampshire

Department of Administrative Services – Vendor Resource Center

www.admin.state.nh.us/purchasing/vendorresource s.asp

New Jersey

Department of the Treasury – Division of Purchase & Property

www.nj.gov/treasury/purchase/doingbusiness.shtml

Vendor Registration

www.state.nj.us/treasury/purchase/erfpnotifications .shtml

Minority & Women Business Enterprise (MWBE) Certification (state program)

www.nj.gov/njbusiness/contracting/minority/certificatio n.shtml

DBE Program

www.state.nj.us/transportation/business/civilrights/dbe. shtm

New Mexico

General Services Administration – Purchasing Division

www.generalservices.state.nm.us/spd/spd.html

DBE Program

www.nmshtd.state.nm.us/main.asp?secid=11175

New York

Office of General Services - Procurement Services

www.ogs.state.ny.us/purchase/default.asp

Minority & Women Owned Business Enterprise Program (state program)

www.nylovesmwbe.ny.gov/Certification/Overview/Ove rview.htm

North Carolina

eProcurement Services

http://eprocurement.nc.gov/

Vendor Registration

www.ips.state.nc.us/ips/vendor/vndpubmain.asp

DBE Program

https://apps.dot.state.nc.us/vendor/directory/

North Dakota

Procurement Office

www.nd.gov/spo

Vendor Registration

www.nd.gov/spo/vendor/registry/

DBE Program

www.dot.nd.gov/divisions/civilrights/dbeprogram.htm

Ohio

State Procurement

http://procure.ohio.gov/proc/index.asp

Minority & Small Business Certification (state program)

www.development.ohio.gov/dmba/minoritysmallbusine sscert.htm

DBE Program

www.dot.state.oh.us/Divisons/EqualOpportunity/Pages/DBE.aspx

Oklahoma

Department of Central services

http://ok.gov/DCS/Central_Purchasing/index.html

Vendor Registration

www.ok.gov/DCS/Central_Purchasing/Vendor_Registration/index.html

DBE Program

www.okladot.state.ok.us/regserv/dbeinfo/index.htm

Oregon

Department of Administrative Services - Procurement Office

www.oregon.gov/DAS/SSD/SPO/index.shtml

Minority, Women & Emerging Small Business Programs (state program)

www.oregon.gov/OBDD/OMWESB/index.shtml

DBE Program

www.oregon.gov/ODOT/CS/CIVILRIGHTS/sbe/dbe/dbe_program.shtml

Pennsylvania

Department of General Services

www.dgs.state.pa.us

Rhode Island

Procurement & Vendor Information

www.ri.gov/business/index.php?subcategory=21&linkgroup=91

Small Business Enterprise Services (state program)

www.mbe.ri.gov

South Carolina

Procurement & Vendor Information

http://sc.gov/Portal/Category/DOINGBUSINESS

Small & Minority Business Enterprise Program (state program)

www.govoepp.state.sc.us/osmba/apps.html

DBE Program

www.dot.state.sc.us/doing/dbe_quarterly.shtml

South Dakota

Office of Procurement Management - Procurement & Vendor Information

www.sd.us/boa/opm/vendor_info.htm

DBE Program

www.sddot.com/operations/dbe.asp

Tennessee

Department of General Services Purchasing Division

www.tennessee.gov/generalserv/purchasing/dobusi.html

Diversity Business Enterprise Program (state program)

www.tn.gov/businessopp/index.html

DBE Program

www.tdot.state.tn.us/civil-rights/smallbusiness/

Texas

State Purchasing & Vendor Information

www.window.state.tx.us/procurement/

Historically Underutilized Business (HUB) Program

www.window.state.tx.us/procurement/prog/hub/

DBE Program

www.dot.state.tx.us/business/business_outreach/dbe.htm

Utah

Department of Administrative Services – Purchasing &Vendor Information

http://purchasing.utah.gov/vendor/index.html

Vermont

Business & Vendor Information

http://vermont.gov/portal/business/index.php?id=92

DBE Program

www.aot.state.vt.us/CivilRights/Dbe.htm

Virginia

Total e-Procurement Solution

www.eva.state.va.us/vendors/index.htm

Department of Minority Business (DMBE) Program (state program)

www.dmbe.virginia.gov

Washington State

Access – Business & Vendor information

http://acccess.wa.gov/business/dobus.aspx

Vendor Registration

http://access.wa.gov/business/state_start.aspx

State Office of Minority & Women's Business Enterprise (state program)

www.omwbe.wa.gov

West Virginia

Purchasing Division

www.state.wv.us/admin/purchase/

DBE Program

www.state.wv.us/redirect/wvdot/wvdot.htm

Wisconsin

Bureau of Procurement

http://vendornet.state.wi.us/vendornet/default.asp

Certification Central (WISCert Central) for small, disadvantaged, minority, women and veteran (SDMWV) businesses (state program)

http://commerce.wi.gov/BD/BD-Wiscert.html

DBE Program

www.dot.wisconsin.gov/business/engrserv/dbe-main.htm

Wyoming

Administration & Information - General Services Division

http://ai.state.wy.us/GeneralServices/Procurement/index.as
p

CHAPTER 4

Key Elements Enhance Success

Winning Aspects to Emphasize

Not all grant application submissions are persuasive to reviewers, nor are they all funded. Obviously, some grant applications are more successful than others. It is certainly important that the grant application be written as clearly and succinctly as possible. Most granting agencies will be receiving more applications than they can possibly fund. Later in the book, there will be a detailed discussion about how to construct a winning grant proposal.

Certain elements enhance success. One of these is **fiscal accountability**. Can your non-profit concretely demonstrate that it has in place the necessary fiscal accountability measures that will ensure that the granting agency's dollars will be spent exactly as specified in the grant application? Private foundations may and the government will audit most non-profits receiving funding. Even governments are audited. For example, the federal government audits state governments to ensure that the money was spent as specified.

How can you demonstrate fiscal accountability? In some applications there will be direct questions about this issue. Don't brush off these questions with a cursory answer. Provide as much detail as possible about how these grant funds will be segregated from other funds that the non-profit receives. It is of particular interest to auditors how the non-profit will track personnel costs identified in the grant application. The non-profit may be asked to supply pay stubs.

Do not apply for multiple government grants if the non-profit does not use the services of an outside accounting firm to audit the non-profit's books. An independent audit is of the utmost importance. The actual amount changes over time but any non-profit receiving more than $500,000 from government grants must have an outside auditor.

Unit Costs

Think of the funding organization, whether public or private, as a smart shopper. The reviewers are looking at unit costs. Private or public raters will be comparing how much product, services or outputs of some kind, can be produced among the competing applications. If your non-profit has the capacity to inexpensively deliver a particular program or service because it creatively uses volunteers or interns, then the non-profit should emphasize that fact in the grant application. Non-profits, where the personnel costs are high because of expansive benefits such as health insurance or retirement plans, are at a disadvantage when it comes to unit cost comparisons unless they have some other factor that minimizes these high costs. However, this alone should not discourage potential grantees from applying since the delivery of high quality, innovative or highly effective programs is important to reviewers. Cost is not the only factor.

Collaborations

Most public and private granting organizations, in their cost cutting mind-sets, need to make every dollar count so collaborations become extremely important. Some grant applications will demand the existence and functioning of collaboration as an eligibility criterion. The eligibility criteria will spell out exactly the composition of the collaborators. For example, in a health-related research project the collaborations could be among a local government entity, a private or public institution of higher learning and a non-profit that can conduct effective community outreach. Usually these collaborations don't exist so they need to be constructed for the purposes of the grant. By submitting the grant application to the granting organization certain demands must be met. Most commonly, the members of the collaboration must have written agreements spelling out the exact responsibilities of each member of the collaboration.

Non-Profit Acts as Fiscal Agent for Individuals

Collaborations are often the best tool for individuals seeking to obtain grant funding. For the non-profit it is an opportunity to utilize the talents and services of an individual often by treating them as a sub-contractor or specifically acting as their fiscal agent. Most government granting agencies do not permit individuals to submit applications. For the non-profit this can be a low cost alternative to having or hiring specific staff for a project or program. Private funders also permit a small or mid-size non-profit to be treated as a contractor and a large non-profit to act as the fiscal agent. This allows a smaller organization to leave the fiscal accountability and many personnel issues to a larger organization to manage. No organization acts as a fiscal agent without some form of financial remuneration. Usually this translates into the large organization receiving some type of indirect cost from the grantor organization (5-20% of the total grant award).

Criteria

How does a grantor organization, public or private, determine the value of a grant submission? Some private foundations, usually the largest ones, and most government grantors develop a point system that allows them to grade each application. Most government grants are reviewed by career civil servants or recognized experts based on written criteria located within the RFP or announcement. Information required in the grant application is often assigned specific points. The actual point system will change from grant to grant, public agency vs. private foundation. However, the concept is universal. All government grantors and most large foundations need to have a reasonable objective and formal review systems in place. An actual rating sheet will be created for each applicant. Under the Freedom of Information Act the rating can be made available to the public in the case of government reviews.

A good hint for estimating the number of actual reviewers (excluding online applications) is the requirement of how many copies of the grant application to include in the submission. If you are required to send three, four, or perhaps even six copies, the number reflects the number of reviewers involved in the process.

Be sure to carefully read how the point system is allocated. For example, a recent Health & Human Services grant on Sexually Transmitted Diseases had only two categories: Plan Description (60 points) and Capacity (40 points). There were only a few questions pertaining to each of these statements in the Criteria section of the announcement. However, in the body of the RFP there were a series of far more detailed questions. It then becomes the challenge of the grant writer to incorporate all the other discussion points into these two major criteria described in the RFP.

It is quite common to have the RFP list five, six, or even more specific criteria. Typically, NIH lists five criteria: significance, approach, innovation, investigator and environment. Many NIH RFPs list the five criteria but don't specify a numerical point system. Instead, the RFP states that the reviewers will make the determination. However, the RFP will provide information on the expected "Objectives and Scope" of the proposed program/project. The areas of interest to NIH are provided in the RFP as examples of studies that are more likely to be funded.

A recent state agency RFP was incorporated a model design format. Each selection criteria was clearly listed (there are seven); and the issues to be addressed for each criteria were given. In addition, the point system was placed on the page next to each criterion listed so immediately the grant writer can determine where the reviewers are expecting the strengths of the submission to be placed. In this case, the greatest importance rested with budgetary issues.

When preparing drafts of the submission, keep reminding yourself which criteria the reviewers are emphasizing. On the draft page write the points assigned to each criterion. Imagine that you are writing a critical essay and the professor assigns points to each portion of the essay. You can get partial credit for an answer.

Family foundations and smaller private foundations do not have an elaborate point system such as the ones utilized by the big foundations or government agencies. However, the vast majority of corporate foundation grant applications do include a series of detailed questions that must be addressed as part of the application process.

Don't Agree To More Than the Non-profit Can Handle

Never commit to more than your non-profit can complete during the grant period. This is a common mistake of inexperienced applicants. If the RFP requires that the non-profit provide services for up to three distinct categories of populations such as minorities, women or geographic areas with high rates of a specific disease, don't automatically conclude that your non-profit must provide coverage for all three populations. There are no extra points by the reviewers if your plan is expansive, especially if the reviewers don't think the non-profit can deliver on its promises.

CHAPTER 5

Judging the Future Based on Past Performance

History & Accomplishments

Why should a private or public granting organization trust your non-profit with grant money? How is your non-profit structured and what has it accomplished in the past? These are questions that need to be addressed in any grant application.

These factors are important to weave into the basic narrative of the project. Private and public grant reviewers are not looking for Pulitzer Prize winning narratives; yet the case must be made that your non-profit has the experience, the necessary staff and the capacity to achieve the goals and objectives written in the grant application.

In the case of faith-based organizations, it is often essential for both private and public funders to understand the separation of the religious mission from the ability to deliver programs or projects. There are a number of foundations totally dedicated to providing funding to religious organizations. The Foundation Center provides information about those specific foundations.

If it can be done, introduce the non-profit's official mission statement into the narrative, especially if it incorporates a compelling reason for the existence of the non-profit.

Uniqueness

It is common for an agency to receive far more applications than it could possibly afford to fund. What's one way to present an appealing and winning case? What about if your non-profit is unique? Is it long-established? Is it the first in the neighborhood? Were the founders special in some measurable way? If the non-profit serves a special population: minorities, women, the disabled, or former prisoners; are members of these populations represented on the Board of Directors? Are staff also members of these special populations which the program/project is designed to serve? Does the non-profit follow a specialized training such as day care centers that utilize Montessori techniques or the center is a member of the National Association for the Education of Young Children (NAEYC)?

It's best to find something – anything that presents a uniqueness that separates your non-profit from the many others. Essentially in the grant application, the grant writer is creating a marketing plan that demonstrates some degree of uniqueness.

Past Accomplishments

The best proof of the non-profit's ability to succeed is to analyze what the non-profit has done in the past. Does the non-profit have an enviable track record? Can the reviewers pinpoint examples of past accomplishments that will lead them to expect similar results if they award a grant to the non-profit? Again, the grant application will probably not ask direct questions about past accomplishments, but it will indicate places where the information needs to be introduced.

The best method of demonstrating a track history is to build a story line. When did the non-profit start offering this service or a complimentary one? It is interesting to note if the non-profit started in a specific way and then proceeded to alter its course because of obstacles. This is a mark of a flexible and dynamic non-profit. No non-profit operates a program or service without problems.

If the non-profit offers a large number of different services, its only necessary to provide a line or two about those services. The grants writer wants to focus on past accomplishments that prove or demonstrate that the non-profit is capable of meeting the current grant requirements. Do not fill up the pages with superfluous information. The reviewers neither have the time nor the inclination to read pages of fluff. Focus on what the non-profit has done in the past that has a direct link to its ability to do something similar in the future.

If the non-profit has never done the specific service or program requested in the RFP, a different approach is necessary. Then the story line has to move in another direction. Why now is the non-profit capable of entering into a new service or program? Where specifically in its history are there similar links? Did the non-profit add new staff with a new set of expertise? Did the non-profit initiate new collaborations that allow it to enter into new territory? Did the community change and its needs shift? Is the non-profit moving with the community towards offering new programs and services?

The past accomplishments must be very specific. It's not enough to just indicate the non-profit did this or that. Give dates, places, numbers served. Does the non-profit have press stories that support its accomplishments? Don't send copies of the press reports; weave the information into the story line. Valuable attachments are letters of support from community leaders, other non-profits, political figures that support past accomplishments and the potential of the non-profit to achieve the goals and objectives in the application. It is always easier to draft a letter of support and then they can modify the letter to reflect their own style.

If the non-profit has successfully received government grants then it's important for the new reviewers to know that information. The easiest way to display that information is by creating a simple table with the vital information such as the following: grant title, amount, which grantor government agency, short phrase on purpose, and dates.

Staff Distinctiveness

Does the non-profit's strength arise from its staff? The easiest way of demonstrating the non-profit can meet the goals and objectives of the grant application is through the utilization of specific staff. Many grant applications will request job descriptions and resumes to accompany the application if funding is being sought for personnel. Those should be included whether or not they are requested as attachments. However, that's not enough. It is important to emphasize the skills, education, and experience of specific staff in the body of the grant submission. It should be emphasized that it's these skills that will make it possible for the non-profit to achieve the aims of the grant application. Not only are the past important accomplishments of the non-profit to be stated, but also the past achievements of specific staff. Do they have awards or press stories worthy of noting? Do particular staff members have interesting personal stories to weave into the grant application as supportive documentation?

The tricky issue is when there is no specific staff in place. Non-profits may wait until the funding is available before they go out and hire staff. If this is the case, then it is the job description that becomes important as demonstrating proof of potential new accomplishments.

Capacity to Meet Program/Project Goals and Objectives

This is the selling point. Will the non-profit be able to meet its obligations? What is there about this non-profit, as opposed to other non-profits bidding for the dollars that assures the reviewers the money will be well spent? There may be direct questions about this issue and the grant application must address them head on with specifics. The specifics include fiscal accountability, past accomplishments, service to the community, staff distinctiveness and measurable/reasonable goals and objectives.

Unlike most foundation or corporate grants, the government is rarely interested whether the project is sustainable after the funding period. Government funding is usually multi-year and so it is expected that the program or service will continue for the three or five years of the funding cycle. The government doesn't assume the non-profit will continue a program or service in the absence of continued government funding. However, most private funders ask how the non-profit will continue the funded program/project after the grant money is spent. If there is potential for revenue (e.g., fees for classes, corporate sponsorships) then that should be noted. Or perhaps a new fundraising campaign will be initiated after the grant period. If this is a possibility then it should be noted.

If sustainability is an issue among government funders, it's because the government grant money serves as seed money. For example, if the state government provides grant funds to create or expand a day care center or a charter school, then it is expected that funding must be available after the initial period.

CHAPTER 6

What's the Problem?

Why Should This Project/Program be Funded?

Unlike private foundation grant applications where the problems may be quite vague, government grants usually address specific issues and problems. In the RFP description, there may be pages of explanation why the government is interested in this problem. There is nothing to be gained by restating the obvious. However, a good grant application will succinctly describe how it is specifically addressing what may be a national or state problem.

Statement of Need

The "Statement of Need" section is the justification for why the project/program should be funded. It may or may not be directly addressed as a specific targeted part of the criteria; but regardless, it must be discussed. This section is where the grant applicant describes the community that will be served by the grant funding. The description of the problem must be very specific to the location chosen. Many corporate foundation grants ask questions about a statement of need and what specific geographic area is to be covered by the grant submission. Most corporate foundations fund grants where the corporation has operations or the bank has branch offices. So the geographic area where the grant will be having an impact is important and must be identified.

The grant application should identify physical, economic, social, financial, institutional or other problems that will be addressed by successful funding of the application. If possible create maps that pinpoint the actual geography. In a government RFP the granting agency will discuss the purpose of the RFP, and within this description will be the key dimensions to emphasize in a "Statement of Need" section. For example, in a recent federal RFP on childhood obesity, the statement of the problem was clearly provided. "Research has shown that obesity in childhood tracks into adulthood, carrying along with it increased susceptibility to hypertension, dyslipidemia and glucose intolerance. In fact, the striking increase in the prevalence of childhood obesity over the past 30 years has been associated with a marked increase in the incidence of type 2 diabetes among adolescents."

So, the Statement of Need has to directly address two issues. First, demonstrate that the community has a problem by providing statistics concerning overweight children, adolescents with type 2 diabetes, adults with diabetes, etc. Also consider how the statistics have changed over the past ten or twenty years. Second, the program described in the application must be designed to meet this problem with specific interventions that are effective. Statistics should be included that identify successful interventions. If the program being considered in the grant application is entirely novel or innovative then there must be statistics to indicate positive change will occur. There must be hints or possibilities described in the literature that point in this direction. Using reputable references is important; actual citations from acceptable professional or scientific journals are encouraged.

Use of Demographics

Every grant application should contain some type of demographic information. The best comparisons are between the subject area and the larger community. For example, if the area under consideration is a zip code, compare this zip code with the city or county, the state and the nation if it makes the problem more pressing. Comparisons should always be included, but carefully choose which statistics make a better case. It isn't that statistics lie, but some present a more compelling story.

The most effective way of demonstrating the power of demographic analysis is graphically. It is a true adage that in using demographic information, "a picture is worth a thousand words." The easiest approach is to create graphs and tables that visually tell the story without much explanation. Microsoft's Excel software is a useful tool. It is easy to insert these tables and charts into the text if you're using Microsoft's Word software. There are many better, more sophisticated statistical packages that produce beautiful charts and tables, but may not be as easy to use. Word combined with Excel software does a nice job. The writer doesn't need to have any real knowledge of statistics or demographics to use the Excel software.

The most common graphic charts in the Excel software are column, bar, line and pie. Personal choice can determine which type of graph or chart is used, but remember that reviewers will probably be seeing the application and its attachments in black and white. Applications are usually reproduced for reviewers on black and white printers or copiers.

The Excel software column graph selections include: cluster, stacked, 100% stacked and then 3D visual effects. Again, unless the intent is to include all copies with color graphs, the 3D Versions can be distracting. The bar graphs are similar to column graphs except that the information is displayed horizontally rather than vertically. For information that looks at points over time such as monthly clinic visits over a year, daily arrests during the week, a line graph is a good pictorial choice. Using the line graph, Excel lets you then compare the geographic area under consideration with some other geography such as a city, county, state or the nation. A pie chart is also a favorite choice. It's usually easy to read and a means of displaying information in a highly descriptive manner. Practical examples of using pie charts are describing the ethnic/racial backgrounds of an area's population or results of a customer satisfaction question. The best looking pie charts use color, so remember that fact in using them in a grant application. As always when working with any type of charts, never overwhelm the reader with too many categories. It's best to keep things simple.

Where To Go

Where does the non-profit find reliable demographic information on items such as age, race/ethnicity, income, poverty rates and gender? Begin with local government sources. Most cities and towns maintain some demographic information on their community for use by the local Planning and Zoning Board. All state agencies also maintain detailed information on the state either in the Planning Department or through the Economic Development Department. Every school district maintains detailed information about the school body: overall population of school-aged children, race, ethnicity, poverty (eligibility for free lunch), school progress, descriptions of the child's household.

The best single source of all demographic data is the US Bureau of the Census. The web site is www.census.gov. Look for the Census Bureau's "American Factfinder." After you locate that site, click on "Fact Sheet." This is a remarkable site for almost an unlimited amount of information on a large variety of demographic subjects such as population, housing, poverty, education, income, commuting to work, migration, etc. The problem is that it is not a particularly user friendly site. It takes experience to maneuver through the many sources of specific information. The 2010 Census material has been analyzed by the experts and is available (a full count of the population is conducted every ten years as required by the US Constitution). In addition to the ten year census, the US Census Bureau conducts a wide range of yearly surveys that measure economic activity, housing statistics, migration-immigration figures and overall population. The Bureau of the Census publishes yearly estimates of the population.

Other great sources of demographic information vary depending on the type of the information. For example, the federal Department of Justice is the place to go for crime statistics. There is a sub-agency that collects data of all kinds. For medical and disease information the sources are The Centers for Disease Control & Prevention (CDC) or National Institutes of Health (NIH). The federal Department of Labor surveys and publishes a wide range of labor, employment, occupational information.

Competitive Analysis – Who Else is Doing This

Although a RFP may never directly ask about anyone else in the community is doing what your non-profit's grant application is proposing, inevitably this is an issue. Think of the grant application as a product which will be compared to other similar products in the marketplace. If you consider the application as a marketing plan for the project/program, then assume two forms of competition: other applicants and other existing non-profits or programs in the community not requesting funding. There is a fear by private and public funders of encouraging unnecessary duplication of services.

As a part of the "Statement of Need" material, include information about other programs or non-profits that are doing similar activities in the community where the program is proposed. It is rare that the activity in your proposal is unique in the community. Should this actually be the case, then make certain that the uniqueness of the program itself is prominently discussed in the grant application. If there are programs in the community that appear similar, the grant application must concretely describe how the applicant's submission is somehow different and superior to what is already available. Emphasizing the improved nature of the program is the key in effectively marketing the value of the non-profit's application.

Demonstration or Pilot Program

Requests for applications that specifically seek "demonstration" or "pilot programs" are truly gifts. Search out RFPs that have these twin words – demonstration project or pilot project in the titles. It usually means that the common way of dealing with this problem isn't working. The private and public funders have decided because a problem may be new or so long-entrenched that something totally innovative is needed. It is then the non-profit's challenge to show that it has the talents, experiences or expertise that lends itself to successfully diving into something new. The non-profit that has a reputation for successfully fostering change in the community or solving intractable problems is a viable candidate for a successful award, even if it does not have a track record with the private or public funding sources.

CHAPTER 7

The Body of the Grant Application

Tell the Story Concisely but with a Compelling Message

A grant application consists of several parts and all of them are essential in order for the grant to be even considered by reviewers. Think of the application as a book comprised of chapters. However, each chapter does not carry equal weight in a point system developed by the reviewers. Before diving into the application read and re-read the description that is the framework for the program narrative. Within the RFP, there is often a discussion of the problem or need -- the reason for the RFP. The private and public funders have decided to fund the RFP because it has accumulated information that leads it to believe there is a problem that needs to be solved.

The inclusion in a government RFA of specific government sources of information reflects the government's previous investment. It is recommended that the non-profit, even if it is familiar with the problem, search out those references and read them. Valuable information is usually contained in the sources. If the RFP provides direct web site linkages to source material then the reviewers expect applicants to be familiar with the source material. If possible, use the source material in the program narrative. Inclusion of this material indicates that the applicant is familiar with the information. If possible, refer to or directly quote the source material as a justification for the application submission and the non-profit's ability to be successful at tackling the problem.

Program Narrative

The Program Narrative is the backbone of an application submission. In many cases, the grant application will require the inclusion of a section labeled "Program Narrative." There is no standard template that the non-profit can use for this section. However, the rationale for the application submission is contained in this section.

Instructions

There are always instructions that accompany the "Program Narrative" section. Follow the instructions precisely. The instructions often require seemingly insignificant requisites but pay attention to all of them. Typically these instructions include: maximum length of the document, paging, font size, spacing and margins of each page, non-profit's name on each page or the opposite -- no name on the pages. If the document is not sent electronically then there will be requirements about the number of copies as well as original signatures.

The page length requirement for the "Program Narrative" is a very important starting point. There are rarely a minimum number of pages required but often the maximum is clearly stated. The page length of the Narrative varies dramatically. (Applications can be as short as 2-3 pages or as long as 50 pages.) In general, private and corporate foundation grant application submissions are less lengthy than government applications. Usually the amount of money being requested is considerably different. Typically, a federal government grant applicant is seeking funding of at least $25,000 while private or corporate grant requests can be as small as $500. Large major foundations have an application and page requirements similar to the government in both size and scope.

Program Narrative requirements vary in complexity. Large major foundations and the government are more similar while family, private and corporate foundation Program Narratives are generally simple and straight forward. As a rule, the "Program Narrative" section is open to the interpretation of the submitting applicant. There may be some questions to be addressed but few can be answered with just "Yes" or "No." The narrative is a like a school paper – it is left to the imagination of the writer to describe the problem, specifically indicate how to solve it, and follow-up with a plan on how to evaluate the success of the venture.

Executive Summary

Sometimes the "Program Narrative" requires the inclusion of an Executive Summary, Program Summary or an Abstract. Write the summary last because then it will be easier to summarize the proposed program/project. The request for an Abstract may also include restrictions; usually it is framed as a summary description of 250 words or less. Use the 'Word Count' tool in Microsoft's Word software to ensure that the Abstract is the proper length.

The Executive Summary usually has restrictions. Typically, the summary should be one page in length or no more than two pages. As always with any given restrictions, follow them precisely.

Key Sections

One can expect that the "Program Narrative" should contain information on the need for the program/project. However, there may be a distinct and separate section called 'Statement of Need'. Then there is the marketing of the non-profit; why your non-profit is the perfect instrument for solving the problem. This is usually followed by a detailed discussion of the goals and objectives and the specific actions the non-profit will undertake to implement the goals and objectives.

Usually a "Program Narrative" will also require some kind of 'Evaluation Plan'. The government and major foundations will require a detailed evaluation plan. Sometimes the federal government has hired an outside firm to conduct the evaluation. The applicant just needs to budget for the costs associated with contributing to the evaluation (i.e., personnel, data collection, and time allocation). Private and corporate foundations will require an evaluation but it can usually be conducted internal to the non-profit organization and at a minimum cost.

If the non-profit does not have the expertise to write a grant application, and is so cash strapped that it is unable to pay for the services of an outside grant writer, you may be able to actually fund the grants writer through providing funding through the evaluation plan. In some instances an effective grants writer can also serve as the evaluator.

A "Program Narrative" may require a 'Management Plan'. Here it is important to highlight the specific talents, experiences and expertise of all the individuals involved in the program/project. The 'Management Plan' may require providing organizational charts with designated lines of authority.

Also, Program Narratives can have quirky requirements. One may require a 'Table of Contents' especially if the narrative is lengthy. Others require the completion and inclusion of special tables and charts. Some narratives permit the grant writer to reconstruct a table or chart to make it easier to complete if there isn't any way to electronically access the table. State government grant applications are particularly lengthy if the funding agency expects many small and mid-size non-profits to apply for funding. Experience has demonstrated that smaller non-profits can have difficulty completing all the actions they promised in their grant application. So to ensure that the work is done on time and within budget, the state funding agency will require the completion of many forms and ask many questions.

Prepare an Outline or Check List

This is a suggestion, particularly for a non-profit that has never previously applied for outside grant funding. Start by reading and diagramming the essential points described in the RFP. Create a check list that includes questions you may have as you read the grant application.

Most funders, private and public, will answer your questions about the grant application and the process. The contact names for private or corporate foundations are usually located on the foundation's web site. There may also be a phone number provided or an email address.

Most government grant applications include the name(s) of contact people (phone number, email address).

These people are your new best friends. You cannot pester these people with repeated questioning. But as part of the check list you should compile a list of questions and submit it to the contact people at one time. The federal government often has a proscribed "Comment Period" during which you can submit your questions regarding the grant application or the process. Beyond that comment period the government will not accept questions. If the government grant application required or permitted a Letter of Intent, all questions received and answered will be automatically forwarded to your non-profit. The outline can assist the grant writer in determining what specific information is required, where in the application to insert the information or demographic tables as well as what attachments should be included in constructing a successful application.

The outline is a guide in constructing the winning and compelling story about the program/project. It need not be elaborate but it should assist the grant writer in the construction of the Program Narrative.

Actually, some grant submissions require the completion and inclusion of a prepared "Checklist" while others simply include a checklist as a guide to the grant writer.

Goals and Objectives

This section is often hastily constructed resulting in the program/project being rejected. Consider this section as the tool which reviewers go through and determine whether the program/project is feasible. The goals and/or objectives, (different funders use a different terminology but with the same intent), are essentially the plan on how the non-profit intends to meet the problem addressed earlier in the Program Narrative.

If the information in the RFP speaks to the funder's specific goals and objectives, such as increasing financial literacy or reducing violent youth gang crime, then the grant submission should include addressing the funders' goals. Most government funders provide referenced information in the Announcement section of the RFP, the sources cited are usually government reports that mention the federal or state's overall goals and objectives. If you can incorporate these government goals and objectives into the program/project being proposed, it demonstrates the non-profit's familiarity with the problem.

The RFP expects that the goals and objectives are measurable and can be completed in specific time frames. Sometimes the RFP will suggest or require that this information be detailed in a table format. If possible, even if not requested, construct the goals and objectives in an easy to read table. This will force the grant writer to quickly ascertain the logic of the goals and objectives as well as the actions to be taken. Staring at all the vital information in a table format makes it easier to notice timing issues or the sequencing of events.

A model table can be constructed that lists each goal or objective followed by specific actions that will be taken, when these actions will occur, which individuals will be responsible or involved in the actions, how it will be measured and how it will be evaluated. The timetable can be either be in months or quarters depending on the nature of the grant submission.

Speak to the Language of the RFP

Use the jargon that is cited in the RFP. Private and corporate foundations are less likely to use any jargon. But each government agency has its own specific language and these words need to be repeated in the grant submission. The government is famous for its use of acronyms and assumes that anyone responding to a RFP will be familiar with its use of language. Acronyms and jargon are just shorthand and if you want to join the club then it is expected you are well versed in the language.

Again, if government sources are cited in the RFP, read them and use them in the grant submission. Use information from government sites in developing the goals and objectives section as your non-profit's plan to further the government's goal to reduce a problem or change a situation or create a new environment. In creating the Program Narrative also consider the reviewers stated Criteria in the RFP.

The trick of developing an effective grant application in response to a RFP is thinking like the reviewers. How would you rate the application? Essentially, the grant writer is weaving a good story, using the language of the RFP, reinforcing the funder's interests in certain areas and gaining the most points by effectively building on the criteria enumerated in the RFP. It is often helpful to have an outside person read the grant submission to ensure it is building an effective story and the flow is logical.

CHAPTER 8

Writing the Budget

Does the Non-profit have a feasible financial plan?

Nothing is more essential than a carefully constructed budget based on realistic numbers and a justification for all the dollars requested. Private and corporate foundations do not require highly sophisticated budgets but justification and real numbers for the items to be funded. State government grant budgets usually follow the budget categories of federal government grants.

The federal application process usually requires that specific forms be completed and submitted with the grant submission. Form 424A – 'Budget Information – Non-Construction Programs' is a two page form that is not difficult to complete. However, the tough part is carefully crafting a budget that passes the federal reviewers' feasibility analysis. Has the non-profit created a budget that reflects the costs of developing a program/project and will the award amount permit the successful implementation of the goals and objectives described in the Program Narrative? Instructions for the SF (Standard Form) 424A are provided on-line.

The budget categories or 'object class categories' are listed on the Form 424A. They are ordinary categories one would use in any budget: personnel, fringe benefits, travel, equipment, supplies, contractual, construction, other. This particular form 424A includes a category labeled construction but it is to be used when the applicant is not requesting federal government funding for construction purposes. If construction is required but will be paid by other than non-federal government funding it is to be listed on Form 424A. In the case where the applicant is seeking federal government funding for construction purposes, use Form 424C 'Budget Information – Construction Programs.'

In developing a budget, the two major categories are personnel costs that may represent the majority of the expenses and OTPS – Other than Personnel Services. What is important for private, corporate and federal government reviewers is whether the program can be adequately funded. Does the applicant intend to use other sources of funding beyond the grant including program income – revenue?

Private and corporate funders often assume that the grant funding is only seed money and that the program will last because the non-profit will be able to sustain the program into the future with other fiscal sources. Often these questions are directly asked of the applicant. How will this program be sustained? As a result of viewing the grant as only a one year funded project the budget information submitted is often only a simple Excel software spreadsheet.

The government does not think in the same way. Programs grant funded by either state or federal government sources most often assume that without government funding the program will cease to exist. The grant is often for multiple years and so at a minimum two year detailed budgets are required. There is also often a requirement to estimate budgets for the entire grant funded period (2-7 years depending upon the exact grant).

The online federal grant application requires completion of quarterly budgets for two years. State government grants often follow this same pattern since most of the original money was from the federal government. The easiest method is to simply divide the requested funding by four. However, that approach may not be the most appropriate based on how costs are expected to be spent. Whether or not the budget is assigned a high number of points (20% or more of total points is considered significant) under the selection criteria, government reviewers will carefully scrutinize the budget. Do not be misled by the simple forms, the budget is one of the most decisive pieces of the grant submission.

As of 2005, if the non-profit is receiving $500,000 or more annually in grant funding from the federal government, the non-profit must prepare and submit the infamous A-133 Audit. This is an expensive audit that must be prepared by a highly competent, outside auditing firm familiar with the rules and regulations concerning the A-133 Audit. It is reasonable to expect that the cost of such an audit can range from $20,000-$25,000. The dollar amount triggering an A-133 Audit has been steadily rising. The dollar amount is based on totaling all federal government awards for the year so that two awards of $250,000 apiece will trigger the A-133 Audit.

Personnel Services

This is often a key component of the budget for larger grants ($25,000 or more). For small grants (less than $5,000), particularly private and corporate foundation grants, there is no personnel component. The inclusion of personnel costs as part of the grant budget assumes that without adequate funding for personnel the program/project cannot move forward.

In constructing the project/program budget, start with the direct personnel responsible should the non-profit receive funding. If there is an incumbent in the position, typically a grant application will require a resume. If the position is new or vacant, the grant submission should include a job description for each position. In developing the budget, think in terms of position title, percentage of time each position will dedicate to the program/project based on a 12 month period, and the salary/fringe benefits for each position. Then consider how the position will be funded – what sources will the non-profit be tapping to cover the costs of each position. For example, the position of Program Coordinator (title), will be dedicated to the project 100% of the time for 12 months. Now will the Program Coordinator position be funded 100% from this grant submission? Or will the position require funding from other sources such as program revenue, other federal or state funds, or fundraising sources?

WARNING: If the non-profit intends to fund a position from more than one government source, be warned that the decision will raise a red flag for government fiscal reviewers. Government auditors are concerned with the issue of supplanting of government funds. What that means is the government thinks a non-profit is double dipping, paying for the same position twice from two separate government sources.

It is obvious that if a non-profit uses government funds, all expenditures must be carefully recorded; recordkeeping must be of the highest quality. Sometimes a non-profit provides documentation for each piece of equipment purchased and all printing and mailing, but then fails to maintain adequate personnel records. Be certain that personnel pay stubs are kept and clearly indicate the position's time spent on any government funded program/project.

Fiscal reviewers for private and corporate foundations are less strict about accounting practices. However, all funds from grant sources even if the amount is small (less than $5,000) should be segregated from the non-profit's operating accounts.

Indirect Costs

Every government grant application is different regarding the acceptability of including indirect costs in the budget. The finance people in the non-profit will appreciate the value of using indirect costs, but in preparing the budget, read all the fine print concerning this issue. Being able to include this in a grant is considered a gift by most finance people, since it can cover general administrative costs seldom directly funded such as the accounting or legal staff, rental space, utilities and telephone. Private and corporate foundation grants rarely offer in-direct costs.

If the non-profit is receiving or actively seeking government funding for a variety of programs/projects, the finance staff should consider negotiating with the government an acceptable, indirect rate. The advantage of such an agreed upon rate is that if the grant submission permits it, the non-profit simply plugs in the rate. However, if the rate is low then it may not be advisable to always use the same rate for each program/project. This is something the grant writer and the financial staff should discuss.

Also, the indirect cost is usually based on a specific percentage, but with strings attached. For example, the grant may state within the budgetary description in the RFP that an applicant can use an indirect expense of 10 percent. The 10% refers to expenses that have been approved by the government grant fiscal staff. So the non-profit may assume that a grant of $100,000 with an indirect cost of 10% automatically means there is $10,000 to offset the costs of the accounting and legal staff of the non-profit. This is not necessarily true in all cases. If the non-profit purchases a piece of equipment for $5,000 but the government agency fiscal staff rejects that expense (and this can happen), the indirect will be based on $95,000 - $9,500 unless you can find a $5,000 cost that is acceptable to the government fiscal staff.

WARNING – Even if the grant award budget lists equipment or supplies, do not spend the money until the non-profit receives specific, written approval for those items. The most common problem occurs over personnel expenses. An individual may leave the non-profit and there is a vacancy, and subsequently savings in the grant award. Get permission to redirect the personnel money to another purpose before moving forward and spending the money. That can also mean getting permission to pay the salary and fringe benefits of a new hire or a transfer within the non-profit.

In-kind-Costs/Matching Requirements

The mandated inclusion of a matching funds requirement can be a deciding factor in whether to go forward and submit a grant application. A smaller non-profit should read the RFP carefully regarding this issue before moving ahead. Talk with the finance staff. If there is a matching requirement, the fiscal staff needs to carefully examine what types of costs will satisfy the matching requirements. Government grants sometimes have matching requirements especially if it's a construction grant. Private and corporate foundations don't usually have matching requirements if the grant period is only for one year or small (less than $5,000). A matching requirement may be necessary if the grant period is two years or more.

In some cases, a federal government award cannot be matched by another federal government grant or any federal funds, while in other cases there are no restrictions. The tricky part about using other government funds for matching purposes is knowing exactly the source of that funding. For example, state government grant awards are often based on awards from the federal government. If there is restriction on the use of federal funding for matching purposes then check carefully the source of any state or local money. Although the award letter comes from the state or local government award, it may still be unacceptable. The best source of advice for these technical matters is the contacts that are listed in the RFP.

A non-profit can expect that if the RFP speaks about challenge grants, then matching will be required. Challenge grants are issued by private, corporate and government funding sources. The issue is usually that the amount of money the non-profit has to match grows while the foundation or government contribution declines. The purpose in these changing financial requirements is to make the program/project self-sufficient because by design there are potential revenue streams or other fundraising possible. Ordinarily the match must also be actual money and not in-kind.

Restrictions

Private and corporate foundations include restrictions on the types of activities that are permissible to be funded with the grant money. Typically, these restrictions have to do with fundraising activities and sometimes operating expenses.

There are rarely government grants without restrictions. There are two types of restrictions that require careful review by a non-profit. First, restrictions on activities the RFP will fund. These types of restrictions can be activities such as training when the RFP speaks about implementation. If the grant is successfully awarded, it may be that costs associated with training will be rejected. Second, there are usually restrictions on fundable expenditures. Every grant will be different but almost all have some type of budget restrictions. Carefully read what the grant will **NOT** pay for in the RFP. The usual "no-no's" are expenses linked to items such as travel and food (federal grants usually restrict the per person costs for meals). For example, the federal government will not pay for first class airplane travel. The government has an acceptable vehicle reimbursement rate and accepts no other rate. The restrictions can be much more formidable. If there is a question, discuss the issue with the government contact person. There are usually two different types of contacts listed in the RFP; a program contact and a fiscal contact. These people should become your new best friends.

Individuals are commonly excluded from directly receiving grant funding whether it's private, corporate or government funding. However, that restriction can be ameliorated by honest ingenuity. The non-profit organization can function as a fiscal agent for an individual. In other cases using the fiscal agent concept, the individual is hired as a consultant for the program/project.

CHAPTER 9

Rejection

The rejection letter is only the beginning

The government as well as private and corporate funders actually appreciate a non-profit that is willing to try more than once. No is never the end of the discussion. Private sources (private or corporate foundations) are under no obligation to provide information about why the grant was rejected. Most will permit anyone to view those projects/programs that were funded. Usually a corporation will release a press release with the information.

However, the government is under an obligation to provide information about the program/project's rejection. How much information is provided will vary from agency to agency. In some cases, the government reviewers will include a letter detailing the shortcomings of a grant application. If a letter does not provide any specific reasons for the denial, there is nothing lost by making a call or sending an e-mail to one of the RFP contacts listed. The non-profit's first effort may not have secured enough points. A non-profit can ask how many points it earned from the reviewers.

Consider the denial letter as a first step in seeking funding from other grant sources. The non-profit has now gained the experience of applying and should have learned some things about the process or enough of it. The non-profit has an easier time completing all the application forms. In the case of the federal government, the cumbersome on-line process has been completed. A denial letter can provide the basis for the next application.

While we would like to think that if we wrote a more compelling story the grant would have been funded, rarely is it that simple. Most of the time, the rejection has to do with the implementation plan (carrying out the goals and objectives) or the budget. The reviewers did not have faith that the information provided in the grant application was sufficient to assure that the plan would be carried out in a timely fashion. In some cases, the plan was simply not what the reviewers were looking for in an application. The plan was outside the parameters described in the grant guidelines. Other typical shortcomings have to do with budgetary concerns or the expertise/experience of staff.

For the next try, re-examine the budget and look for ways to trim unit costs. The non-profit's staff may earn more experience through a training course or new degree. Look for RFPs or grant guidelines that seem to require similar expertise or areas of interest as the submitted grant application.

Another common problem is the failure to secure the appropriate outside support, if a partnership or coalition was required. This is the time to continue working on creating a more viable group, which can collaboratively apply for more grants.

In many instances, the recipients of funding are listed. There may be a useful description of the actual winning grant applications. Carefully examine the available materials. Look for similar programs/projects but also the geographic distribution of the winning grant applications. Private, corporate and government grantors have a certain obligation to spread around the wealth. If there are no winning applications from your community it can work in your non-profit's favor at a future try. The reviewers probably don't want to neglect a particular area too many times. At the same time, if the community has a very successful model in place there may be no point in re-applying.

It isn't until a non-profit actually competes for private, corporate and government funding that it can truly appreciate the winners. As always with funding, never discount the power of politics. For that reason, it is highly recommended to engage corporate people as volunteers for the non-profit and to have contacts in the offices of local, state and federal representatives.

CHAPTER 10

Non-Profits working with Individuals

Think Collaborations

Grant Funding for Individuals

Individuals working collaboratively with non-profit organizations can effectively win private, corporate and government grants. It the best possible avenue for individuals to pursue and it can be a win-win for the non-profit. Individual artists and scholars/researchers will be attracted to these types of collaborations.

The potential grant awards are really unlimited. The most likely collaborations are between the individual and a college or the educational department of an arts/cultural non-profit. Most museums, orchestras, theater groups even libraries operate educational programs for children, adults, seniors and special populations such as the disabled,, minorities/disadvantaged, and/or immigrants. It is not an accident that visual artists, performers, writers and poets often teach to support their artistic endeavors. Private, corporate and government granting agencies are interested in projects/programs that enhance the learning experience of public school students, including those enrolled in charter schools in grades K-12.

Federal Agencies offer unique opportunities for individuals

The non-profit collaboratively working with an individual artist or scholar/researcher should regularly check on certain federal agency sites for new grant opportunities. Although it may not seem apparent, but a wide range of federal agencies make grant opportunities available through fellowship programs where a non-profit organization acts as the fiscal agent for the individual.

What follows is a brief description of some selected federal agencies that offer fellowship opportunities.

US Department of Justice

There are two programs that scholars with an interest in criminal justice should regularly check at the Department of Justice, Office of Justice Programs, National Institute of Justice www.ojp.usdog.gov/nij. One is the W.E.B. DuBois Fellowship Program and the other is the Graduate Research Fellowships. The DuBois Fellowship seeks fellows to focus on crime, violence, and the administration of justice in diverse cultural contexts. It also requires fellows to spend at least a minimum of 2 months at NIJ, which is located in Washington D.C.

The Graduate Research Fellowships program seeks students at the dissertation stage. It is assumed that the research subsidized by NIJ will lead to a Ph.D. and that the candidate's dissertation committee is fully supportive of the research. The official applicant for these fellowships is the sponsoring academic institution. This is typical of government fellowships. While the financial support is for the individual's expenses, the actual applicant is an academic institution. This is beneficial for the individual because it places the burden of financial accountability on a non-profit accustomed to meeting financial reporting demands.

US Department of Energy

The federal government is highly supportive of research endeavors that increase opportunities for junior academic faculty. The Department of Energy through its Office of Science has funding opportunities for junior faculty in widely diverse subjects. Again the applicant is the academic institution and in this case the supported investigator is a tenure-track physicist.

US Department of Defense

The Department of Defense through its US Army Medical Research and Materiel command operates the Idea Development Award. Independent investigators at all levels are eligible to submit proposals focused on innovative research. The individual conducts the research through an academic institution or research-oriented non-profit organization; and matching is expected from that non-profit or institution.

National Science Foundation

The National Science Foundation lists 21 pages of grant opportunities. Clearly, most are not designed for individuals but included are a variety of Fellowships. The best place to start is with NSF's Web site: www.nsf.gov and click under the heading, "Funding Opportunities."

The Graduate Research Fellowship Program (GRFP) sponsored by NSF lists opportunities in nine general academic categories including life sciences, chemistry, computer and information science and engineering, etc. Each fellowship subject category has similar application procedures but different deadlines. These broad categories cover the vast majority of all academic subjects. The caveats for these fellowships are four: 1) fellowships are awarded only for study leading to research-based master's or doctoral degrees; 2) research with disease-related goals is not eligible for support by NSF 3) clinical and counseling psychology are generally not supported by this program; and 4) the research must include a scientific approach.

In addition, the NSF sponsors other fellowships or research opportunities. The following are just samples of what is available: International Research Fellowship Program, Louis Stokes Alliances for Minority Participation Program, Discovery Corps Fellowships; NSF Directors Award for Distinguished Teaching Scholars, Research Experiences for Undergraduate, GK-12:NSF Graduate Teaching Fellows in K-12 Education. Again the best advice is to check the NSF Web site.

National Endowment for the Arts

The National Endowment for the Arts is the largest annual funder for the arts in the United States. Congress appropriates its funding, which fluctuates with the political currents. Usually there is funding in the $100 million range. NEA then turns around and funds all the states. The result is that overall government (state and federal) funding for the arts is approximately $800 million annually. NEA funds a wide range of organizational and individual grants to all types of artists both established and unknown. In the past, it was a much more generous donor of grants to individuals, but as its money has been restricted, the agency's ability to fund individual artists has been cut. It was once the grantor for highly controversial artists, but that has also changed.

NEA funds small non-profit organizations and the major arts non-profits in the country. NEA awards grants in several categories: dance, design, folk and traditional arts, literature, media arts, music, musical theater, opera, theatre and visual arts in addition to museums, presenting (concert series), multidisciplinary and local arts agencies (other than state agencies).

NEA National Heritage Fellowship awards are $20,000 and ten are awarded each year. The awards are meant for master folk and traditional artists. The grant funding is also awarded through a nomination process and the individual must be nominated by another person or non-profit.

National Endowment for the Humanities

The National Endowment for the Humanities is a federal agency which funds grants that enhances and expands on the study of the humanities. The term humanities refers to language, (both modern and classical); linguistics; literature; jurisprudence; philosophy; archaeology; comparative religion; ethics; the history, criticism and theory of the arts; those aspects of social sciences which have humanistic content and employ humanistic methods; and the study and application of the humanities to the human environment with particular attention to reflecting on our diverse heritage, traditions and history.

Although the subjects of the grant awards are in the realm of the humanities, the medium used can also be radio or television. Individuals working through a non-profit can apply for what NEH labels: Radio Projects: Consultation Grants; Radio Projects: Development and Production Grants; Television Projects: Consultation Grants; and Television Projects: Planning, Scripting or Production Grants.

CHAPTER 11

In Conclusion

Awards Keep Coming Regardless of Economic Times

Good luck with writing your grant proposal. There are opportunities out there for non-profit groups of all kinds. Do not get discouraged if your proposal is rejected; remember the advice from the first line of this book. The United States government has billions of dollars earmarked for grants. With determination and a well-organized proposal, your grant proposal can succeed.

Private, corporate and government priorities shift so that grant opportunities never disappear but changes are likely. A new CEO, the retirement of a long-time foundation head or a new federal administration or a new Congress can set new priorities. There will never be enough funding to meet every request by the thousands of non-profits in the country.

The best approach is to design a funding strategy that looks at the many varied potential sources of funding that a non-profit can successfully obtain. A well-constructed and comprehensive strategy requires understanding that funding must be diverse especially if it's directed at a specific proposal or program. The following are only suggestions:

- Federal Government

- State Government

- City/County/Local Government

- Corporate Foundations

- Private Foundations

- Family Foundations

- Individual Donations/Sponsors

- Revenues – Bidding for Government Contracts

Searching for funding support is more an art than a science and it is a wise approach to look everywhere. While the internet is becoming the tool to use for researching where to find grants, unfortunately, it is does not capture all grant application information.

The non-profit needs to find someone (best case scenario a volunteer or intern) to review all the announcements and information that is available. A knowledgeable person must read through the materials to determine whether the grant announcement is something worth pursuing. Use this book as a resource while researching and writing a proposal. We live in a fast paced world so be prepared and nimble as you cast out a net for potential sources of private, corporate and government grant funding.

Grant & Contracting Glossary

Explanation of Grant & Contracting Terminology

Acquisition is the acquiring of supplies or services by a government agency with appropriated funds through purchase or lease.

Applicant is the entity requesting a grant.

Applicant notice is published on Grants.gov and invited applications for one or more discretionary grant competitions. It provides basic program and fiscal information on each competition, informs potential applicants when and where they can obtain applications, and cites the deadline date for a particular competition.

Application Package is a group of specific forms and documents for a specific funding opportunity which are used to apply for a grant.

Assurances are a variety of requirements, found in different Federal laws, regulations and executive orders, which applicants agree in writing to observe as a condition of receiving federal assistance.

Authorized Organization Representative (AOR) is the individual who submits a grant on behalf of a company, organization, institution or government. Only an

AOR has the authority to sign and submit grant applications.

Award is financial assistance that provides support or stimulation to accomplish a public purpose. Awards include grants and other agreements in the form or money or property in lieu of money, by a grantor agency to an eligible recipient. The term does not include: technical assistance, which provides services instead of money; other assistance in the form of loans, loan guarantees, interest subsidies, or insurance; direct payments of any kind to individuals; and contracts.

Benefits.gov is a federal website created in 2002 to provide citizens with easy online access to government benefit and assistance programs. Information provided includes on citizen tax filing, federal rulemaking, electronic training, and benefit information delivery.

Budget period is an interval of time into which a project period is divided for budgetary purposes.

Budget narrative explains the budget. Explanations can include the derivation of amounts, the itemization of totals, the purpose of purchased supplies and services, and the justification of the size of salaries, fringe benefits, and indirect costs.

Catalog of Federal Domestic Assistance (CFDA) lists all domestic assistance programs of the Federal Government. It includes information about a program's authorization, fiscal details, accomplishments, regulations, guidelines, eligibility requirements, information contacts, and application and award process. It is maintained by the General Services Administration. It can be found on the web at http://12.46.245.173/cfda/cfda.html.

Certificate of Competency is a certificate issued by the Small Business Administration (SBA) stating that the holder is "responsible" in terms of capability, competency, capacity, credit, integrity, perseverance, and tenacity for the purpose of receiving and performing a specific government contract.

Certified 8(a) Firm is a firm owned and operated by socially and economically disadvantaged individuals and eligible to receive federal contracts under the SBA 8(e) Business Development Program.

Contractor Team Arrangement is an arrangement in which (a) two or more companies form a partnership or joint venture to act as potential prime contractor; or (b) an agreement by a potential prime contractor with one or more other companies to have them act as its subcontractors under a specified government contract or acquisition program.

Cost sharing or matching is the portion of project or program costs not borne by the grantor agency.

Deadline date is the date by which a discretionary grant application must be received by a grantor agency in order for it to be considered for funding.

Discretionary grant is an award of financial assistance in the form of money by a grantor agency to an eligible grantee, usually made on the basis of a competitive review process.

DUNS Number is a nine-digit number assigned to an organization by Dun & Bradstreet (D & B) and required to successfully transmit electronic on-line federal grant applications.

E-Business Point of Contact (E-Biz POC) is responsible for the administration and management of grant activities in his/her organization. The E-Biz POC authorizes representative of their organization (AOR) to submit grant applications through Grants.gov. An E-Biz POC must also register as an AOR to submit an application.

Emerging Small Business is a small business concern whose size is no greater than 50 percent of the numerical size standard applicable to the Standard Industrial Classification (SIC) code assigned to a contracting opportunity.

FedBizOpps.gov is the single point-of-entry for commercial vendors and government buyers to post, search, monitor and retrieve opportunities solicited by the entire federal contracting community.

Federal Acquisition Regulation (FAR) is the body of regulations which is the primary source of authority governing the government procurement process. The FAR, which is published as Chapter 1 of Title 48 of the Code of Federal Regulations, is prepared, issued and maintained under the joint auspices of the Secretary of Defense, the Administrator of General Services Administration, and the Administrator of the National Aeronautics and Space Administration.

Federal register is a daily compilation of Federal regulations and other Federal agency documents of public interest including competitive grant proposals prepared by the National Archives and Records Administration.

Funding Opportunity Announcement is a publicly available document by which a federal agency makes known its intentions to award discretionary grants or cooperative agreements, usually as a result of competition for funds. Funding opportunity announcements may be known as program announcements, notices of funding availability, request for proposals, solicitations or other names depending on the agency and type of program. Funding opportunity announcements can be found at Grants.gov/FIND and on the internet at the funding agency's or program's website.

Funding Opportunity Number is the number that a federal agency assigns to its grant announcement.

Grant is an award of financial assistance, the principal purpose of which is to transfer a thing of value from a grantor agency. A grant is distinguished from a contact, which is used to acquire property or services for the grantor's direct benefit or use.

Grantee is an individual or organization that has been awarded financial assistance by a grantor agency.

Grants.gov is a storefront web portal for use in electronic collection of data (forms and reports) for federal grant-making agencies through the Grants.gov site (www.grants.gov).

Indirect cost rate is a percentage established by an agency for a grantee organization, which the grantee uses in computing the dollar amount it charges to the grant to reimburse itself for indirect costs incurred in doing the work of the grant project.

Local Government is a local unit of government, including specifically a county, municipality, city, town, township, local public authority, school district, special district, intro-sate district, council of governments, or any other regional or interstate entity.

Marketing Partner ID (MPIN) is a personal code that allows you to access federal government applications and acts as your password. You make up the code and register it in SAM. The MPIN must have 9 digits containing at least one alpha character (must be in capital letters) and one number (no spaces or special characters permitted).

North American Industry Classification System (NAICS) Code is a code with a maximum of six digits used to classify business establishments. This code will be replacing the Standard Industrial Classification (SIC) code.

Organization is a grant applicant who is submitting a grant on behalf of a company, state, local or tribal government, academic or research institution, not-for-profit, or any other type of institution.

PDF is a file format designed to enable printing and viewing of documents with all their formatting (typefaces, images, layout, etc.) appearing the same regardless of what operating system us used, so a PDF document should look the same on Windows, Macintosh, Linux, OS/2.

Point of Contact (POC) is an individual who is designated as the person responsible for authorization and maintenance of information on behalf of a registrant, coordinating communication among organizations.

Profile is applicant information stored in the Grants.gov system for the purpose of identifying a user.

Project Period is the period established in the award document during which awarding agency sponsorship begins and ends.

Request for Application (RFA) is a type of solicitation notice in which an organization announces that grant funding is available, and allows researchers and other organizations to present bids on how the funding could be used.

Request for Proposal (RFP) is a solicitation made, often through a bidding process, by an agency or company interested in procurement of a commodity, service or valuable asset, to potential suppliers to submit business proposals.

Small Business Innovative Research (SBIR) is a grant/contract designed to foster technological innovation by small businesses with 500 or fewer employees. The SBIR contract program provides for a three-phased approach to research and development projects: technological feasibility and concept development; the primary research effort; and the conversion of the technology to a commercial application.

Standard Form 424 (SF-424) Series Forms include the following:

SF-424 (Application for Federal Assistance cover page)

SF-424A (Budget Information Non-construction Programs)

SF-424B (Assurances Non-construction Programs)

SF-424C (Budget Information Construction Programs)

SF-424D (Assurances Construction Programs)

Third Party In-kind Contributions is the value of non-cash contributions provided by third parties. Third party in-kind contributions may be in the form of real property, equipment, supplies and other expendable property, and the value of goods and services directly benefiting and specifically identifiable to the project or program.

33048611R00065

Made in the USA
San Bernardino, CA
22 April 2016